True Tales of the Wild West

American Cowboys

Jeff Savage

Enslow Publishers, Inc.

40 Industrial Road
Box 398
Berkeley Heights, NJ 07922
USA

http://www.enslow.com

Original edition published as *Cowboys and Cow Towns of the Wild West* in 1995.

Library of Congress Cataloging-in-Publication Data

Savage, Jeff, 1961–
  American cowboys : true tales of the wild West / Jeff Savage.
        p. cm. — (True tales of the wild West)
  Includes bibliographical references and index.
  Summary: "Discusses American cowboys, including the origins of cowboys, their
day-to-day lives, cattle drives, cow towns, famous cowboys, and their importance to
the Wild West era in American history"—Provided by publisher.
  ISBN 978-0-7660-4019-9
  1. Cowboys—West (U.S.)—History—Juvenile literature. 2. Frontier and pioneer
life—West (U.S.)—Juvenile literature. 3. West (U.S.)—History—Juvenile literature.
I. Title.
  F594.S27 2012
  978'.02—dc23

2011026331

Paperback ISBN 978-1-4644-0027-8

ePUB ISBN 978-1-4645-0475-4

PDF ISBN 978-1-4646-0475-1

Printed in the United States of America

092011 Lake Book Manufacturing, Inc., Melrose Park, IL

10 9 8 7 6 5 4 3 2 1

To Our Readers: We have done our best to make sure all Internet addresses in this book
were active and appropriate when we went to press. However, the author and the
Publisher have no control over, and assume no liability for, the material available on
those Internet sites or on other Web sites they may link to. Any comments or suggestions
can be sent by e-mail to comments@enslow.com or to the address on the back cover.

♻ Enslow Publishers, Inc., is committed to printing our books on recycled paper. The
paper in every book contains 10% to 30% post-consumer waste (PCW). The cover
board on the outside of each book contains 100% PCW. Our goal is to do our part to
help young people and the environment too!

Illustration Credits: From *The American West in the Nineteenth Century: 225
Illustrations from "Harper's Weekly" and Other Contemporary Sources*, first published
by Dover Publications, Inc., 1992, p. 7; Enslow Publishers, Inc., p. 23; © Enslow
Publishers, Inc. / Paul Daly, p. 1; Library of Congress Prints and Photographs, pp. 9,
13, 17, 25, 31, 38, 41; © North Wind / North Wind Picture Archives, p. 29; Peter
Newark American Pictures / The Bridgeman Art Library, p. 36.

Cover Illustration: © Enslow Publishers, Inc. / Paul Daly.

Contents

chapter 1

The Night Watch

I t was so dark that James McCauley couldn't even see the horse he was sitting on. It was cold, too. James had always wanted to be a cowboy, but he didn't like standing guard over a bunch of cattle in the middle of the night.

James and his cowboy friends were driving a herd of cattle up the trail to Montana by day. Now they were asleep. Everyone, that is, except James and his buddy, Scandlous John. It was their turn to be night guards.

James could not see the hundreds of cattle all around him, but he could hear a few of them eating the grass. Most of them were sleeping. Scandlous John was at the other end of the large herd, some distance away. James was tired of sitting on his horse. He was a little scared of the dark, too. This was his third night standing guard, and it wasn't any easier than the first two. James kept thinking about his empty bedroll back at camp. He couldn't wait for the next guard to take over in an hour so he could get some sleep.

At about nine o'clock, a black cloud came down from the northwest. Raindrops began to fall. Good thing James was wearing his slicker. The rain came down harder and harder, and soon it was pouring. What a terrific storm! Lightning flashed and thunder clapped. "All at once," James recalled, "the steers got on their feet and in less time than it takes to tell it they was gone."[1]

James's horse had been trained to stay with the cattle, and so it raced off after the herd with James still in the saddle. The young cowboy was caught in the middle of a stampede. He couldn't see. He didn't know what to do. At every crack of lightning and boom of thunder, the herd jumped in fright, changing direction. James held tight to his horse. Some of the cattle ran down a ravine. Others went up and over a hill. James went wherever his horse took him. This craziness continued for two hours.

When the rain had finally stopped, the storm passed, and the moon came out to light the ground, James could see that most of the cattle were gone.

They had run off and were scattered across the countryside, no telling where. Scandlous John was gone, too. Worst of all, James was lost.

The young cowboy saw that he had about three hundred cattle still with him. After things quieted down, the cattle lay down to sleep. James rode off to see if he could find the camp. He didn't want to wander too far from the rest of the herd, though, so he returned shortly. He had no idea where the camp was.

Stampedes were very dangerous for cowboys. Thunder and lightning often caused cattle to stampede, but any loud noise could startle them.

James had grown up on a farm in the East, dreaming of someday becoming a cowboy. He had no idea it would be like this. Barely eighteen years old and on his very first cattle drive, he was sitting on a horse with three hundred sleeping cattle at his feet, lost in the dark wilderness. How would the other cowboys ever find him? James got an idea. If he could make a loud enough noise, maybe they would hear him back at camp. James drew his six-shooter from its holster and pointed it in the air. Bang! The cattle jumped to their feet, and away they went.

"Now I had more trouble than if I had let things alone," James said when retelling the story some years later. After chasing the cattle for an hour, he managed to settle them down again. Then he climbed off his horse, lay down in the grass, and fell asleep.

The next day he wandered for miles on his horse. Finally, through sheer luck, he found the other cattle drivers. Scandlous John had been found, too.

Young James McCauley's real troubles were yet to come. After a few days and nights on the trail in heavy storms, the cowboys and cattle arrived at the Arkansas River. The Arkansas was so wide and deep that the cattle drivers had to travel alongside it for three or four days in search of a place to cross. There were no

Cowboys had a tough job. Stampedes were just one of the many dangers they faced during a long drive. James McCauley learned the hard way. This cowboy sits on his horse in a photograph taken around 1888.

bridges, of course, in the wilderness of the Wild West. Finally, the trail boss decided to send everyone across.

James rode carefully down the bank on his horse and entered the river. The water came up to his horse's knees, its stomach, its neck. Soon, the horse's nostrils were all that was left above the water. Halfway across, the river got even deeper. The whole horse went under. James was sent floating down the river in a strong current. At the last possible second, he grabbed hold of a steer.

"I got him by the tail," James said, "and away we went for the other side." James reached safety, but he had lost his horse and everything he owned—his saddle, bridle, blankets, and spurs.

He rode bareback on a spare horse for a week until the cowboys reached Pueblo, Colorado. There, his friend Scandlous John surprised him with a new saddle. Eventually, the cowboys arrived at their destination—Miles City, Montana. James was so relieved. He had survived the cattle drive. He had become a true cowboy. Even so, he figured he was through being a cowboy. "I promised myself that I'd never go up the trail with a herd anymore," he said. "Swimming them rivers was just a bit too dangerous for me."

James McCauley broke his promise to himself. He did go on several more cattle drives, and some were just as hazardous as the first. James couldn't help himself. You see, he got a certain magical feeling out of being a cowboy, a feeling that he couldn't get from farming or ranching or schooling. And so that's what James wanted to be—a cowboy.

chapter 2

The American Cowboy

In the mid-1800s, the United States was like two different countries. The eastern half—from the Atlantic Seaboard to the Mississippi River—was bustling with activity. Its cities boomed with factories, like the new steel mills in Pittsburgh, Pennsylvania. Horse-drawn trolleys clogged the busy streets. Train tracks spread from town to town like a maze of connect the dots. The western half—from the Mississippi and across the Rocky Mountains to California—was almost desolate. The region between the Rocky Mountains and the Mississippi was drier and flatter than either coast and appeared useless. Geography books at the time referred to it as "the Great American Desert."

Easterners had little interest in this vast expanse, also known as the Great Plains, except for spots where gold was discovered. One Easterner who crossed the plains in 1846 wrote: "No living thing was moving . . . except the lizards that darted over the sand. . . . The level monotony of the plain was unbroken as far as the eye could reach. Sometimes it glared in the sun, an expanse of hot, bare sand."[1]

Easterners missed one crucial element of the area—grass. The plains were covered by nutritious wild grasses. More than 40 million buffalo once roamed this rangeland, feeding off the grasses. Most of the buffalo were slaughtered for their hides, leaving the grassland empty. It was the perfect place to raise cattle.

The First American Cowboys

Some of the first American cowboys were American Indians. Cattle were brought to the New World by Christopher Columbus, who placed them on the island of Santo Domingo in 1493. In 1521, hundreds of cattle were transported to mainland Mexico.

More than one hundred sixty years later, cattle were driven north of the Rio Grande into what is now the United States. American Indians were trained to be cowboys at the missions the ruling Spanish had established there. These American Indian cowboys were called *vaqueros*. They rode short-bodied horses and tended large herds of cattle that were raised for their hides and for tallow, the fat used to make soap and candles.

As the United States expanded westward, settlers from the East came into contact with the Mexican and American Indian vaqueros and their vast herds of cattle. Soon, they established their own ranches.

The first American cowboys, called vaqueros, were American Indians.

Pork vs. Beef

Pork had long been the choice of meat for Easterners, but around the time of the Civil War (1861–1865), beef became more common in the diet of many citizens. Thousands of cattle were scattered across Texas, and Easterners had an interest in them. The trick was getting the cattle to the Eastern cities.

Only two railroads stretched westward across the plains. One was the Union Pacific Railroad; the other was the Missouri Pacific Railroad. These railroads were more than a thousand miles north of southern Texas. Skilled ranch hands were needed to round up the cattle and drive them north to the railroad towns. From there, the cattle could be shipped by train to the beef-hungry East. With the start of the first drive north, the cowboy was born.

A New Kind of Cowboy

Where did these cowboys come from? Everywhere. Some came from Mexico and points south. Others were African Americans, who had been slaves on Texas plantations. Still others were American Indians, many of them sons and grandsons of vaqueros.

Former Union soldiers from the Civil War made up a large portion of the cowboys, but there were even more former Confederate soldiers, still upset about losing the war. Union and Confederate soldiers, working together on ranches and cattle drives, were forced to get along with each other.

Some came from the East, where they had become bored with domestic life and had heard tales about the exciting West. Others came from as far away as Europe. Some were in search of excitement; others were running away from home.

"My first wishes and desires was to be a wild and woolly cowboy," James McCauley remembered. "The more I saw of them drifting west, the more determined I was to be a cowboy."[2] James had always been teased at school. One day, when he could no longer stand it, he stabbed a bully in the ribs with a knife. He raced home before the authorities arrived, kissed his mother good-bye, and ran off to the West.

Women Cowboys

Though uncommon, women played a role as cowboys. For the most part, women worked as ranch hands, keeping watch over the herds and rounding up cattle. It was often on their own family's ranch. Usually, when a father or husband would die, families thought it quite natural for a woman to help with the farmwork. Few participated in the long drives to the railroads.

In general, though, people did look down on women performing tough farmwork. But during the Civil War, many women took over their ranches and farms when the men left to fight. Finding dresses impractical for such duties, women wore cowboy boots and culottes. Some even wore men's clothing. For the most part, this was done out of practicality. Women had ridden sidesaddle for centuries. Now they rode astride.

The seeds of independence were sown into the hearts of western women. Though many returned to their traditional roles after the war, some women continued to work in ranching. Women achieved a new sense of equality. This would have long-lasting effects. Before women throughout the United States won the right to vote in 1920, they were already doing so in all states and territories west of the Mississippi except New Mexico.

Tools of the Trade

The life of the cowboy was simple, and the cowboy's needs were few. Nevertheless, there were still some indispensable tools of the trade. The first of these was

One of the most important tools for cowboys was a lasso, or lariat. They used this rope to lasso cattle by the neck or horns. It also worked for other purposes as well.

a horse. Distances were great, and without a horse it would be impossible to round up, brand, and drive cattle. For a cowboy, horses were not just transportation but also part of their identities.

Another vital tool was the rope, also known as the *lasso* or *lariat*. Its primary use was to lasso cattle by the neck or horns. But the rope had many other uses, such as dragging firewood, pulling a cow out of a mud bog, or even as a hangman's noose.

Almost all cowboys owned a gun. However, few ever used it for anything more than target shooting.

Some cowboys thought carrying a gun made them more of a man. Many would strap on a holster with a six-shooter to pose for photographs to send to friends and relatives back home. In truth, many cowboys were afraid of even handling a gun. This didn't prevent them from bragging, however.

One cowboy from Montana returned home from town with a bandage on his hand. He bragged that he had been involved in a saloon fight and that the other combatant had been injured far more seriously. His family later found out that the poor cowboy had accidentally shot himself when a photographer handed him a gun so he could pose looking tough.

Character

As much as cowboys didn't mind bragging, they hated to hear complaining. It was considered unprofessional. When a cowboy complained, others would either ridicule him or walk away. There was no sympathy for a whining cowboy.

There was plenty to complain about, too. Ranch work was difficult, and cattle driving under the blazing sun was even harder. It took great skill and courage to push herds of cattle across treacherous territory.

Cowboys could also be vain. Their appearance was important to them, and they would spend as much as fifty dollars—more than a month's wages—on a pair of custom-made boots and twice that on a hat.

Cowboys weren't always well thought of. Some ranchers even avoided using the word *cowboy* and, instead, called them *hands*. Most people in the East thought cowboys were a crazy bunch of gun-toting, drunken hoodlums who caused more trouble than they were worth. That is because most Easterners didn't know any real cowboys.

One man who did know cowboys told a reporter for the *New York Tribune* in 1884, "Cowboys are a much misrepresented set of people. I have taken part with them in roundups, have eaten, slept, hunted and herded cattle with them, and have never had any difficulty. . . . There are many places in our [Eastern] cities where I should feel less safe than I would among the wildest cowboys in the West."[3] The man who said this was President Theodore Roosevelt.

chapter 3

Blazing New Trails

Charles Goodnight had a plan. While most Texas cowboys in the spring of 1866 were preparing to drive their herds north to Kansas and the Union Pacific Railroad, Goodnight looked west. He would open a new trail that would go southwest to the Pecos River, then north through New Mexico into Colorado. When the thirty-year-old cowboy went to town to gather supplies, he met Oliver Loving, a fifty-four-year-old cattleman who knew the land well. Loving frowned at the dangers of Goodnight's proposed route but liked the challenge. "If you will let me go," Loving said, "I will go with you."[1]

Charles Goodnight was resourceful. He had learned as a boy to locate water by watching swallows, to stop thirst by sucking a bullet, to stop hunger by chewing tobacco (the harmful effects of tobacco weren't known at the time), to judge the freshness of a hoofprint by counting the insect tracks on it, as well as other tricks.

The two men set out with eighteen riders and about two thousand cattle. They reached the Concho River without a problem, but the difficulty was yet to come. Twenty cowboys would have stood little chance against the numerous bands of American Indians that lived in Texas and New Mexico. Fortunately, Goodnight and Loving did not encounter any of these bands.

Unfortunately, they also did not encounter any water for days. It was eighty miles from the Concho River to the Pecos River. By the third day, they still hadn't reached their destination. One by one, cattle fell from the herd, collapsed, and died. On the fourth day, as they approached the Pecos, the remaining herd could smell water. The cattle were exhausted, but their instinct was to run, and they stampeded five miles to the Pecos. Two hundred died in the rush to the water, and one hundred more were crushed in the river.

Despite the losses, the drive made plenty of money. Half the remaining herd was sold at Fort Sumner, a reservation of Navajo and Apache in southern New Mexico. The other half was sold to a cattleman near Denver, Colorado. Goodnight packed his saddlebags with twelve thousand dollars in gold.

The partnership ended less than a year later when Loving died of the wounds he received in a battle with a Comanche war party on the Pecos River. But the route that he had helped make famous would forever be known as the Goodnight-Loving Trail.

Trails West and North

Goodnight, however, wasn't the first to try bringing cattle west. The Gila Trail was developed somewhat earlier with similar difficulty. It skirted along the southern end of New Mexico and Arizona before reaching San Diego and turning north to Los Angeles and San Francisco. American Indians along the trail demanded one dollar per head of cattle to cross their land. If the money was not paid, the American Indians would stampede the cattle.

But the most popular routes remained the northern trails to the railroad. One was an old American Indian and buffalo trail that pioneers had used to enter Texas. It stretched to towns in Missouri, including Kansas City and St. Louis. It was named the Shawnee Trail.

The Chisholm Trail

In 1867, shrewd cattle broker Joseph G. McCoy built hundreds of large corrals in a Kansas town called Abilene. Then he convinced the railroad company to stop its trains there. He hoped to lure cowboys to his new "cow town." The plan worked. In Abilene's second full season as a cow town, more than one hundred fifty thousand cattle were herded up from Texas. This successful new route wasn't named after McCoy, but after a Cherokee by the name of Jesse Chisholm, who drove wagons up and down the trail so frequently that others soon called it by his name. The Chisholm Trail became the most famous trail of all.

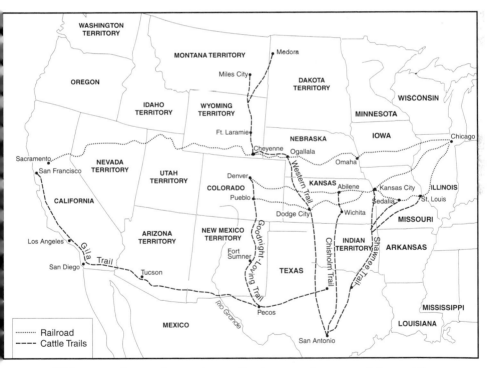

This map shows the major trails that cowboys used for cattle drives as well as the railroad lines that were used to transport the cattle to the coasts.

Roundup

Before cattle could be driven north, much work had to be done. Riders had to be hired and cattle had to be rounded up and branded. The roundup was such a celebration that many townsfolk came to watch the first day.

The roundup often took several weeks. It was difficult to find all the cattle because the grazing land was so vast. One Easterner visiting the West wrote: "On all sides the cattle break away from the main herd, and go tearing back in the direction from whence they came, with the cowboys following in full chase. Up hill, down hill, across the canyon, through brush and water! And such dodging. . . . Why, it's as bad as a flea hunt!"[2]

When the cattle were rounded up and brought to the ranch, the branding began. Many cattle and new-born calves had to be marked with a hot branding iron. This was done in order to identify the owner of the cattle. The branding iron, which was heated in a campfire, couldn't be too hot or it would set the animal's hair on fire. When the hot iron was applied, the cow would cry "*baw-w-w-w-w*!" A brand consisted of a symbol or a group of letters, and each cattle owner had his own brand. One rancher from San Antonio

Before a cattle drive could begin, cowboys had to round up the cattle and bring them to the ranch for branding. This cowboy watches a herd of grazing cattle before beginning a roundup in Genesee, Kansas.

named Samuel A. Maverick depended on an overseer to keep his cattle branded. Legend has it that the overseer was unreliable and allowed the stock to stray unbranded. Most of Maverick's cattle were stolen and branded by others. Stray unbranded cattle, therefore, came to be known as *mavericks*.

chapter 4

The Long Drive

There was nothing more exciting or challenging to the cowboy than the event known as the long drive. It was his chance to show his true cowboy skills. Cattle worth four dollars a head in Texas might be worth more than forty dollars a head in Kansas and Missouri and places north. Driving herds on journeys of a thousand miles or more was a real test of patience, determination, and ability. Cowboys ate dust, wrestled cattle, dodged hostile American Indians, and avoided stampedes. For all this, they made about thirty dollars a month, plus food.

With cattle moving an average of fifteen miles a day, a drive could take several months. The worth of cattle was determined by its weight. "You've no idea how easy it is to knock a dollar off a beef; your profit all depends on moving them along quiet and easy," cowboy E. C. "Teddy Blue" Abbott said.[1]

So many things could go wrong along the way. Cattle could bog down in quicksand or drown in rivers. American Indians could stampede the herd—or worse—if a payment was not made on time. Cattle were easily startled, and thunderstorms could send them running in all directions. Conditions were difficult. Water was sometimes hard to find, food was usually bad, and there was never much time for sleeping. With all of this, why would anyone want to be a cowboy? Because it was thrilling. "I was a cowhand looking for adventure," cowboy W. A. Askew wrote, "and I found it."[2]

The Trail Boss

Once on the trail, the trail boss took over. He stayed close to the herd while making sure the trail was clear of obstacles and dangers. Point riders rode directly in front of the herd to guide it. They also set the herd's pace. Swing riders and flank riders protected the sides of the herd. Drag riders followed the herd, chasing after strays that ran loose and guiding them back to the group. No one wanted to be a drag rider because they ate all the dust.

The cook was often a person too old to ride a horse every day but who still wanted to go on the long drive. The cook drove the chuck wagon, which held all the food as well as bedrolls and supplies. A cowboy's favorite words were "Come an' git it!" because it meant the food was ready. After eating the same meat and beans for a month, though, the cowboy no longer considered the cook his best friend.

Old Blue

One of the cattle always turned out to be a natural leader on the drive. He would walk in front of the herd, and the other cattle knew never to pass him. Most of the natural leaders were steers, and the most famous of these was Old Blue.

It is widely agreed that Old Blue knew the trail from Texas to Dodge City better than the cowboys did. Charles Goodnight bought him from a man named John Chisum as part of a large herd. Old Blue was four years old when he went on his first drive, and he took the lead the very first day and every day thereafter.

He never spooked at sudden noises and never stampeded. Goodnight was so impressed with Old Blue that, at the end of the drive, he did not sell the steer with the rest of the herd. For the next eight years,

Some cowboys take a break and eat a meal around the chuck wagon. Cowboys often tired of eating the same food every day, usually meat and beans.

on every long drive that Goodnight went on, Old Blue was in the lead. A brass bell was hung around his neck, and the rest of the cattle learned to follow its sound. Old Blue lived to be twenty years old.

Trouble

Not all cowpunchers were fortunate enough to have a wise steer like Old Blue, however. They could experience plenty of difficulty on the long drives.

Jim Daugherty was only sixteen years old when he led his first cattle drive over the Shawnee Trail.

It would not be easy. The route led through hilly, wooded country with steep-banked streams. Also, the Choctaw in the region objected to herds being driven across their land. Kansas ranchers posed a threat, too. They claimed that cattle from Texas were infested with ticks that caused "Texas fever."

Daugherty and five other riders set out for Sedalia, Missouri. They weren't far along the trip when they learned of trouble ahead. An outlaw gang had killed one cowboy from another drive and scattered his herd. Other trail bosses were holding their cattle back, hoping the danger would clear. But Daugherty told his riders to stay with the cattle while he rode ahead to Fort Scott. There, he made a deal to sell his herd. He then returned to his herd, and the group forged ahead. All at once, about twenty outlaws swooped down on them, shot one of the point riders dead, and stampeded the herd. Daugherty was tied to a tree and beaten.

One of the outlaws yelled, "Hang him!" Luckily, they decided to let him live.[3] Daugherty and the rest of his men buried their dead comrade, then rounded up the cattle. He originally had five hundred cattle, but he could only find three hundred fifty. He rode the remaining cattle the rest of the way to Fort Scott at night and sold them for a small profit.

A cattle drive was a dangerous journey for cowboys. They had to direct the cattle through rugged terrain, fend off American Indian attacks and cattle rustlers, and deal with a constant need of water.

Lost

The first drive for twenty-four-year-old Ben Mayes was embarrassing. He arrived in camp just as the drive began. The trail boss whistled to "move 'em out." The horses and cattle took off in a mad dash. Mayes tried his best to keep up, but eventually he lost sight of everyone. Worse yet, he didn't know where he was. He couldn't find camp for three days. Mayes was relieved when two cowboys found him and led him to camp.

Teddy Blue Abbott got lost, too. He was sent with another cowboy to meet up with Bill Cody at a lake in the sand hills of Nebraska. The pair rode all day—about forty miles. When they reached their destination, Cody was gone and the lake was dry. The two cowboys made camp that night without food or water.

The next morning they started out for another lake, another day's ride away. The result was the same—no Cody and a dry lake bed. "The first day you want a drink awful bad," Abbott said. "The second day you can't think of nothing else—can't talk—can't spit."[4] Abbott and his buddy were rescued the third day by another group of cowboys who were out rounding up wild horses.

Stampede

One of the worst fears of the cowboy was the stampede. Cattle were frightened by any sudden movement—a rat or lizard, a loud noise, lightning and thunder. Cowboys expected to lose about 10 percent of their herd because of stampedes, but the loss was sometimes much higher.

Cowboys from the Mitchell Ranch in the Big Bend region of Texas were sitting comfortably around a nighttime campfire as their large herd rested nearby.

The silence was broken by a low rumble that every cowboy recognized. The rumble grew louder and louder until it was a massive roar. Stampede! For whatever reason, the cattle were out of control and heading straight for a cliff. Hundreds tumbled over the edge to their death before the blanket-waving cowboys could divert their charge and calm the herd.

On a New Mexico drive in 1877, almost one thousand cattle were lost in a stampede. The early morning cry of a donkey sent the herd running. The cowboys quickly mounted their horses and raced off to try to stop the stampede. One ignorant cowboy raced past the herd, then stopped in front of it and held up his hands, yelling "Whoa!" Lucky for him, another cowboy dashed out to save him before he was trampled to death. The cattle stampeded right over a bank into the Pecos River, where nearly a thousand drowned.

Cowboys were excited to start out on a long drive. After months of hard work, they were just as excited to finish it. Their final destination—the cow town— was a welcome sight.

chapter 5

The Cowboy at Play

As a cow town came into sight, the riders would be overcome by a rush of desire. They yearned for better food, drinks, card games, dancing, and general fun. But they had been in the saddle for months, wearing the same soiled clothes, and were filthy from head to toe. So, more than anything else, they yearned for a hot bath.

$1.25 for a Haircut and a Shave

The cowboys would head straight for the hotels with baths. Not everyone got to enjoy the pleasure of hot water right away. Somebody had to stand guard over the cattle. It was agonizing to sit in the saddle and watch the rest of the riders go into the hotels to get clean, then over to the barber for a shave and a haircut. It was even worse to get clean, only to be suddenly called back to duty.

"It was my night off," one cowboy wrote, "and I went in to whoop 'em up; but a big cloud came up after I had paid $1.25 for a haircut and a shave, and I had to go back to the herd and stand guard all night during a severe storm."[1]

Eventually, every cowboy got a chance to enjoy the cow town. And he made the most of it. He took his pay from the trail boss and spent some of it on food, alcohol, and dancing; and if he wasn't careful, he lost the rest in a card game.

While the townsfolk provided much-needed relief for the cowboy, they also did their best to take his money. Town merchants knew how vulnerable the cowboy was. The bright lights and foot-stomping music were a fantastic spectacle to someone who had spent months on the lonely range. The louder and crazier the town, the more money the cowboy would spend. The wildest of these places were the big boomtowns.

Abilene—The First Boomtown

The first boomtown to rise up from the dust was Abilene. Between 1867 and 1872, more than a million cattle went through Abilene. It was a true cow town. The next cow towns to spring up in Kansas were

Newton, Ellsworth, Wichita, and Caldwell. But possibly the rowdiest—certainly the most famous—was Dodge City in central Kansas.

Dodge City was spread out along the south side of the Arkansas River, on the Western Trail. The town proclaimed itself the "cowboy capital of the world." It boasted the biggest dance halls and the wildest saloons ever seen. In 1884, the town even held a bullfight to celebrate the Fourth of July. There was so much

A cowboy (left) gets a shave and a haircut inside a tent saloon. After a long drive, cowboys wanted to get clean and find entertainment in the boomtowns. This saloon gave cowboys the opportunity for both.

rowdiness that residents demanded more law and order. Even Sheriff Bat Masterson and Deputy Marshal Wyatt Earp couldn't keep gunfights from breaking out in places like the Long Branch Saloon. After a decade of wild cowboys parading through town, Dodge City ended up with another famous landmark—Boot Hill. Here dozens of victims of frontier violence are buried.

As much fun as cow towns were, most cowboys were eager to return to the ranches. There might not be much to do there in the winter months, but at least they didn't have to worry about running out of money, starving, or getting shot in some barroom brawl.

Cowboys Off-Season

When the roundups and drives were over for another year, those lucky enough to get ranch jobs lived together in grungy bunkhouses at headquarters or at lonely camps on the outer fringes of the range. Work involved tending the cattle or maybe mending a fence—not much else. Some cowboys would become so bored that they would memorize soup-can labels and recite soup ingredients to surprised visitors. Many cowboys would relieve their boredom by drinking or playing cards; but most ranches, like the famous XIT spread in western Texas, forbade alcohol and card

When winter ended, cowboys were eager to get back to work. One of their first jobs was bronco busting. In this Frederic Remington print, a cowboy rides a bucking bronco.

playing, at least while cowboys were on the job. Those cowboys who didn't get ranch jobs found work in town doing odd jobs like painting or digging ditches.

Busting Broncos

As the snow thawed and winter gave way to spring, cowboys were excited to be put to work. A typical job was bronco busting. Horses hadn't been ridden for months, and the younger horses had never been ridden. It was the job of cowboys to somehow climb aboard these wild horses and "break" (tame) them. Even Theodore Roosevelt, who would become president of the United States, busted broncos when he was a cowboy. One day, the horse he was riding pitched and bucked so violently that Roosevelt had to "pull leather" (grip the saddle horn with his hand), a technique that was not admired by other cowboys. He managed to stay in the saddle, even though he lost his hat, his eyeglasses, and his six-shooter.

There were plenty of other jobs in the spring, including hauling firewood, planting crops, and rescuing cattle from bogs. When time came for the roundup, cowboys were overjoyed. They were tired of ranch work, and the roundup meant the long drive wasn't far behind.

chapter 6

Trail's End

The Homestead Act was a special act of Congress that made public land in the West available to settlers on payment of a small fee. In return, the settlers had to live on and cultivate the land for a minimum of five years. The people who took advantage of this opportunity were called homesteaders. They marked off their property—160 acres—with fences. Cowboys watched in despair as these homesteaders crept farther and farther westward into the cattle ranges. As "the Great American Desert" became more settled, grazing areas began to disappear. Cattle trails were interrupted. Driving cattle across people's land was declared illegal.

The advent of barbed-wire fences made cowboys more expendable. Barbed wire served as a barrier for grazing cattle. Cowboys were provided with a new duty—fence riding—patrolling the many miles of barbed wire to keep it in good repair. But cowboys were no longer needed for their bigger job of searching for stray cattle. Unless, of course, one managed to slip through the barbed-wire fence.

Train routes eventually came south, and it became unnecessary to drive cattle north. Cattle were simply loaded aboard trains and shipped by rail to their destination.

In 1885–1886, a severe winter storm hit Kansas, Colorado, and the Texas Panhandle, which further crippled the cowboy business. Thousands of cattle froze to death, or were so disabled that they fell victim to predators. Many ranchers sold their businesses to

A group of homesteaders pose for a photo in front of their sod house. The Homestead Act allowed many Americans to claim plots of land in the West. As homesteaders traveled west, the cowboy's way of life was threatened.

cowboys in northern states. The following winter, another vicious storm struck, this time in the north. The worst blizzard in Montana's recorded history hit in January 1887. Cowboys could not leave the bunkhouse for weeks. Untold thousands of cattle froze to death, many while standing up. Hundreds of ranchers were ruined. Most lost their enthusiasm. Cowboying would never be the same.

Yet for a generation, from the end of the Civil War until the mid-1880s, the cowboy rode high. He didn't know it at the time, but he would come to represent the great hero of America. The cowboy took on the rigors of the Wild West, tamed beasts, forged across dangerous wasteland, and carved out his place in American history.

There are still cowboys today. They still ride horses and rope and brand calves. But they have many other chores, too. They may drive to work in a jeep or a pickup truck. They may drive the herd in a trailer-truck. They may even round up cattle with a helicopter. They may repair fences, oil windmills, fix pumps and engines, and drive a tractor. But cowboys today still work with pride. They can tip their hats to the cowboys of yesterday—the cowboys who tamed the Wild West.

Chapter Notes

Chapter 1. The Night Watch

1. Quotes in this chapter excerpted from Ron Tyler, *The Cowboy* (New York: William Morrow and Company, Inc., 1976), p. 166.

Chapter 2. The American Cowboy

1. William H. Forbis, *The Cowboys* (Alexandria, Va.: Time Life Books, 1973), p. 21.

2. Ron Tyler, *The Cowboy* (New York: William Morrow and Company, Inc., 1976), p. 201.

3. Ibid., p. 10.

Chapter 3. Blazing New Trails

1. Ron Tyler, *The Cowboy* (New York: William Morrow and Company, Inc., 1976), p. 89.

2. William H. Forbis, *The Cowboys* (Alexandria, Va.: Time Life Books, 1973), p. 52.

Chapter 4. The Long Drive

1. Ron Tyler, *The Cowboy* (New York: William Morrow and Company, Inc., 1976), p. 80.

2. Ibid., p. 81.

3. Don Ward, *Cowboys and Cattle Country* (New York: American Heritage Publishing Co., Inc., 1961), p. 40.

4. Ron Tyler, *The Cowboy* (New York: William Morrow and Company, Inc., 1976), p. 80.

Chapter 5. The Cowboy at Play

1. William H. Forbis, *The Cowboys* (Alexandria, Va.: Time Life Books, 1973), p. 52.

Glossary

bunkhouse—The place where cowboys slept on ranches off-season.

chuck wagon—A wagon brought along on the long drive to carry supplies and provisions. From here, meals were served to the cowboys.

Civil War—The war fought between the northern states (the Union) and southern states (the Confederacy) from 1861 to 1865. Many cowboys were veterans of the Civil War.

cowboys—The men and women who worked on cattle ranches in the West, particularly those who participated in the long drives.

cow town—Usually a town at the end of a cattle trail, where the herds were sold and packed into freight cars to be sent east.

drag riders—These cowboys followed the herds, protecting the rear and chasing after strays.

flank riders—The cowboys who rode alongside the herd, preventing cattle from straying.

hands—The name some ranchers preferred to call their cowboys.

Homestead Act—An 1862 act of Congress that allowed settlers to obtain public lands. The land would become theirs if the settlers lived on the land for five years and improved it.

homesteaders—Settlers who received land according to the laws of the 1862 Homestead Act.

lariat/lasso—A rope cowboys used to catch runaway cattle.

long drive—The journey made by cowboys and their herds from their grazing lands to the railroads. The drives would cover up to 1,000 miles, and take two or three months to complete.

missions—The Spanish set up religious missions throughout the southwestern United States to convert the American Indians to the Roman Catholic religion. The city of San Antonio, Texas, had its beginnings as such a mission.

point rider—The cowboys who rode ahead of the herd. They set the pace of the drive, kept the herd from spreading out too thin, and looked out for trouble ahead.

stampede—A mad rush of cattle or other herd animals.

swing rider—The cowboys who rode alongside the herd, preventing cattle from straying.

trail boss—The leader of a cattle drive.

vaquero—Spanish for cowboy. The first cowboys in the United States were Spanish settlers and American Indians trained by the Spanish.

Further Reading

Books

George-Warren, Holly. *The Cowgirl Way: Hats Off to America's Women of the West.* Boston: Houghton Mifflin Harcourt, 2010.

Lassieur, Allison. *The Wild West: An Interactive History Adventure.* Mankato, Minn.: Capstone Press, 2009.

McIntosh, Kenneth. *Saloons, Shootouts, and Spurs: The Wild West in the 1800s.* Broomall, Pa.: Mason Crest Publishers, 2011.

Price, Sean. *Crooks, Cowboys, and Characters.* Chicago: Raintree, 2008.

Sheinkin, Steve. *Which Way to the Wild West?: Everything Your Schoolbooks Didn't Tell You About America's Westward Expansion.* New York: Roaring Brook Press, 2009.

Internet Addresses

PBS: The West—Cowboys
<http://www.pbs.org/weta/thewest/program/episodes/five/cowboys.htm>

The Wild West: Cowboy Facts of the American West
<http://www.thewildwest.org/cowboys/wildwestcowboyfacts>

Legends of America: The American Cowboy
<http://www.legendsofamerica.com/we-americancowboy.html>

Index